EGGS

Written By: Anna DiGilio

All rights reserved. No part of this publication may be reproduced, distributed, or transmitted in any form or by any means, including photocopying, recording, or other electronic or mechanical methods, without the prior written permission of the publisher, except in the case of brief quotations embodied in critical reviews and certain other noncommercial uses permitted by copyright law.

For permission requests, write to the publisher:
Laprea Publishing
info@lapreapublishing.com

Website: www.GuidedReaders.com

ISBN: 978-1-64579-536-0

© 2019 Anna DiGilio

Photo Credits:
Cover, Title Page: Depositphotos; IgorVetushko. 3: Depositphotos; Motorolka. 4: Depositphotos; Coprid. 5 (top): Depositphotos; Alkir_dep. 5 (bottom): Shutterstock; PhotoSongserm. 6 (top): Depositphotos; Shershavaja. 6 (bottom): Shutterstock; Jayjued. 7 (top): Depositphotos; Ead72. 7 (bottom inset): Shutterstock; Photographer unknown. 7 (bottom): Depositphotos; Thediver123. 8 (top): Shutterstock; Deb Davis. 8 (top inset): Depositphotos; Lizzylou. 8 (bottom): Shutterstock; Cora Unk Photo. 9: Depositphotos; Igordutina. 10: Depositphotos; Klanneke. 11 (top): Shutterstock; Seasoning_17. 11 (bottom): Shutterstock; Monning27. 12: Depositphotos; YAYImages. 13 (top): Depositphotos; Deerphoto. 14: Shutterstock; Dmitry Lobanov.

TABLE OF CONTENTS

What Lays Eggs?..............................Page 5

Inside an Egg....................................Page 9

Sizes of Eggs....................................Page 12

Glossary..Page 15

What is an egg? It is where a baby animal grows.

What Lays Eggs?

Many animals lay eggs. All birds lay eggs.

Frog eggs

Frogs lay eggs. Toads lay eggs.

Toad eggs

This is a cuttlefish laying eggs.

Fish lay eggs. Sharks lay eggs.

Shark egg

Python egg

Snakes lay eggs. Lizards lay eggs, too.

Inside an Egg

Inside the egg is a yolk. It <u>stores</u> food.

The baby uses the yolk until it <u>hatches</u>.

Most eggs hatch. Babies come out. Then some babies must find food on their own.

Sizes of Eggs

Some eggs are tiny. They can be small as a penny!

Some eggs are huge. They can be the size of a soccer ball!

Ostrich Quail Hen

Take a look. What will hatch from this egg?

GLOSSARY

<u>hatches</u>
(of an egg) opens and produces a young animal

<u>stores</u>
keeps to use later